How Saints Change

Kristina R. Olsen, Ph.D., OCDS

En Route Books and Media, LLC
Saint Louis, MO

Make the time

En Route Books and Media, LLC
5705 Rhodes Avenue
St. Louis, MO 63109

contactus@enroutebooksandmedia.com

Copyright 2025 Kristina R. Olsen
Cover Credit: (front) "The Holy Family Resting" (posted on Wikimedia Commons by Elizabeth Roy on November 7, 2006); (back) Sacred Heart of Jesus as revealed to St. Margaret Mary Alacoque in 1673.

ISBN-13: 979-8-88870-329-8
Library of Congress Control Number: 2025940529

All rights reserved. No part of this book may be reproduced, stored in a retrieval system, or trans- mitted in any form, or by any means, electronic, mechanical, photocopying, or otherwise, without the prior written permission of the author.

For Jesus and for Mary

Table of Contents

Introduction 1

The Blessed Virgin Mary 3

St. Joseph 11

St. Paul (c. 5 – c. 64/65 A.D.) 19

St. Teresa of Avila (1515-1582) 25

St. Padre Pio (1887-1968) 31

Brother Lawrence of the Resurrection

   (1614-1691) 41

St. Mother Teresa of Calcutta (1910-1997) 49

St. Augustine of Hippo (354-430) 59

St. Ignatius of Loyola (1491-1556) 69

St. Francis of Assisi (1181-1226) 79

St. Antony of the Desert (251-356) 87

Conclusion 93

Bibliography 95

Introduction

This book inspires us to invite Jesus to change our lives, by taking a close look at those who have gone before – Christian saints. We show saints from St. Joseph in Jesus' day, up to Mother Teresa of Calcutta in our own time, to see how their reliance on God informed their lives. Let's explore how those who walked closely with Jesus learned to rely on Him wholeheartedly and let's let them inspire us to live truly rich and wholehearted Christian lives.

While we primarily focus on how the saints encountered Jesus and how that led to initial and ongoing conversion of heart, we also consider the context, those around them and other influences that helped them grow, such as reading. In the case of Ignatius of Loyola, two particular books helped him change from a life of worldly knighthood to a focus on being a knight for God, and St. Paul was prepared for his conversion by a thorough knowledge of the Hebrew scriptures.

The book goes through several aspects of how these saints encountered Jesus, whether they had mystical experiences in which they felt that they saw or heard Jesus, or whether they "met" him through the scriptures. These experiences of the saints can help us understand who we are in Christ, and they can encourage us to seek communion, conversation and commitment to Jesus in our own lives.

I hope this book will support your true growth toward union with God and help you live a rich and dedicated life, filled with purpose and harmony in Christ.

The Blessed Virgin Mary

Who She Was

The Blessed Virgin Mary is the mother of God. Jesus was born to her through a miraculous encounter with the Holy Spirit. She was hailed by an angel as "Full of grace." As a mother, Mary cared deeply about her son, and her husband, Joseph. She traveled with Joseph from Nazareth to Bethlehem, where Jesus was born while they were in unfamiliar territory. She hurriedly traveled again with Joseph and Jesus to Egypt, to escape Herod's wrath against a would-be king (Jesus). Again, she lived in unfamiliar territory. Finally, the Holy Family returned to Nazareth, where Jesus grew up.

When Jesus was a young boy, the family traveled to Jerusalem for the Passover feast. Jesus was separated from his parents for three days during their time there, and when his parents found out he was not with their other relatives, they were very worried. They finally found him in the Temple, where he was teaching the elders and other leaders of the Jewish Temple hierarchy.

When Jesus began his public ministry, he traveled to Samaria and other places to teach as a rabbi, and he gathered many followers including his closest disciples, the twelve apostles. As far as we know, Mary stayed at home and was not with her son during this time. Later, when he incurred the wrath of the Pharisees and was sentenced to crucifixion by Pontius Pilate, Mary came to Jerusalem and remained at the foot of the cross during Jesus' time of suffering and ultimately, death.

How She Changed

Mary was a young teenager when we first meet her in the Scriptures. The angel Gabriel visited her and said, "Do not be afraid, Mary, for you have found favor with God. Behold, you will conceive in your womb and bear a son, and you shall name him Jesus. He will be great and will be called Son of the Most High, and the Lord God will give him the throne of David his father" (Luke 1:30-32, *NABRE*).

Mary changed her plans when she first learned of her God-given calling. The angel had also revealed to her that her cousin, Elizabeth, was with child and immediately Mary went to visit her. She stayed with Elizabeth until Elizabeth's baby, John, was born. Elizabeth had previously been believed to be unable to have children, so this was another miraculous event that may have surprised Mary.

Mary was betrothed to Joseph but was not living with him when the angel Gabriel came to her to tell her she would conceive a child by the Holy Spirit. This changed her idea of how her life would unfold – her first child was conceived and born differently than she might have planned, at home with family nearby to help her. Rather, she was far away from home when she gave birth to her son, and she was surrounded with confusion and chaos and people she did not know.

Throughout Jesus' life, Mary had other interruptions in her motherhood. She traveled with her baby to Egypt to save his life from killers sent by Herod. Also, Mary may not have fully understood why Jesus needed to be away from her for so much of his adult life, or why he needed to die the way he did. This would have made Mary not only concerned for her son but also lonely and perhaps depressed at times.

How It Felt

Mary went through a lot beginning at a young age. In the Scripture we are told that she pondered her situation in her heart ("And Mary kept all these things, reflecting on them in her heart" (Luke 2:19, *NABRE*). She was a person of prayer, then, but how did it feel to be thrust into a position of talking to an angel and becoming the mother of God? We are told that she responded, "'Behold, I am the handmaid of the Lord. May it be done to me according to your word.' Then the angel departed from her." (Luke 1:38, *NABRE*). She was accepting of her role as Mother of God, and that may have felt fulfilling for her.

However, she may also have felt stressed, especially since she was betrothed to Joseph at the time and her pregnancy was viewed with suspicion. Her trip to visit Elizabeth – about 80 miles on a donkey – may also have been stressful, leaving her tired, although excited and looking forward to seeing her cousin. Her trips to Nazareth, then to Bethlehem, then to Egypt, and then home to Nazareth again also may have left her feeling uprooted and disoriented for several years.

Later, when she lost track of Jesus' whereabouts in Jerusalem, and ultimately found him in the Temple, she was worried and perhaps angry at Jesus for putting his parents through this. In Scripture we are told Jesus obeyed his parents and went home with them, but also that he was in his Father's house (God's Temple). This dual family of Jesus could have been confusing and problematic for Mary as she sought to have authority over her son.

When Jesus left home and traveled with his disciples, Mary again would have wondered where he was and how he was doing. She may have seen him from time to time, but it is not likely that she traveled everywhere with him. She would have missed him as any mother would, and she was probably worried and eager to see him the next time he came to town.

Finally, when Jesus was sentenced to death, Mary may have felt fear and perhaps anger, as well as bewilderment. She may have felt helpless in the face of the Roman crucifixion of her son. She stayed with him during his time on the cross, up to and including his death. She would have witnessed the Roman soldier piercing Jesus' side with a lance until he bled, to confirm his death. This must have been heartbreaking beyond what words can describe.

After Jesus' resurrection, although it was not recorded in scripture, Mary may have seen Jesus in his glorious body. This would have been a great relief and a joy to her. He appeared to his disciples and then ascended into heaven ("As he blessed them he parted from them and was taken up to heaven" (Luke 24:51)). Perhaps she had wished this could wait so that she could spend more time with Jesus. At the cross, Jesus had asked his disciple John to take care of Mary as his own mother, and he had asked Mary to treat John as her own son. Mary therefore would have felt cared for in her later years through having a son to take care of her, and since she was a woman of prayer she may have felt a special bond with Jesus in heaven even while she was living with John until she died.

What You and I Can Do

What inspires me about Mary is first of all, her fullness of grace. She was already united with God in a unique way due to her Immaculate Conception, in what could be called her pre-redemption from sin by virtue of Jesus' saving work on the cross and his subsequent resurrection and ascension. So, she was already extremely special in her inner life, in her purity and in her relationship with God.

Mary was resilient, strong in faith, dedicated in resolve and focused on taking care of her child and family in the service of God. These are qualities we can take away from Mary's story. I wonder if she did everything perfectly, if she ever burned the dinner or put off doing the laundry. Certainly, she was tired at times. At the Basilica of the National Shrine of the Immaculate Conception in Washington, DC, there is a bronze statue on the lower level that shows the Holy Family resting on the flight to Egypt. In that statue, Mary looks very tired. I always appreciated walking by that statue because it showed an aspect of Mary we don't often see: Mary needed to rest.[1]

---

[1] Anna Huntington, "The Holy Family Resting," https://osjusa.org/st-joseph/art/the-holy-family-resting/

In this depiction of the Holy Family resting during their flight to Egypt, even the donkey looks tired. We can take from this that in the service of God we may be asked to do extraordinary things that take a great deal of effort, but, like Mary, let's remember to rest on the journey.

St. Joseph

Who He Was

Saint Joseph was the husband of the Blessed Virgin Mary. He, along with Mary, was the caregiver for Jesus in his early years. Although he was not his natural father, Joseph was a father to Jesus. Joseph was a carpenter.

The birth of Jesus was complicated. Mary had been betrothed (engaged) to Joseph but she had become pregnant in a miraculous way, through the Holy Spirit's action, before they were married. Joseph was concerned and wanted to call off the engagement. This was considered divorcing her in the Hebrew legal system of that day. But then "the angel of the Lord appeared to him in a dream and said, 'Joseph, son of David, do not be afraid to take Mary your wife into your home. For it is through the holy Spirit that this child has been conceived in her'" (Matt 1:20, *NABRE*). This convinced him to accept Mary as his wife, and Jesus as his son.

How He Changed

An angel of the Lord was a messenger from God. As a result of this angelic visitation, Joseph changed his mind from divorcing Mary, to accepting her and her child and taking them both into his home. According to Pope Paul VI, Joseph "surrendered his whole existence to the demands of the Messiah's coming into his home." This change "becomes understandable only in the light of his profound interior life. It was from this interior life that 'very singular commands and consolations came, bringing him also the logic and strength that belong to simple and clear souls, and giving him the power of making great decisions - such as the decision to put his liberty immediately at the disposition of the divine designs.'"[1]

The power of a single dream caused Joseph to change his direction and surrender his life to the

---

[1] John Paul II, *Redemptoris Custos,* https://www.vatican.va/content/john-paul-ii/en/apost_ exhortations/documents/hf_jp-ii_exh_15081989_redemptoris-custos.html, No. 26, quoting Paul VI, *Discourse,* March 19, 1969.

needs of the Messiah, and to Mary, his mother. This was a dramatic shift.

For Joseph, "divine intervention occurred in a dream three times. The first time was when he discovered his wife's pregnancy. The second time was after the Magi left. The last time was during the return from Egypt." According to John Chrysostom, God did not need to cause an apparition to appear in reality to St. Joseph, as he did for Zachariah, the shepherds, and the Virgin Mary, because "this spouse's faith was strong. He did not need an apparition."[2]

Joseph had a second dream in which an angel warned him to take Jesus and Mary and flee to Egypt: "When they had departed, behold, the angel of the Lord appeared to Joseph in a dream and said, 'Rise, take the child and his mother, flee to Egypt, and stay there until I tell you. Herod is going to search for the child to destroy him.' Joseph rose and took the child and his mother by night and departed for Egypt." (Matt 2:13-14, *NABRE*).

---

[22] Msgr. Dominique le Tourneau, To Know St. Joseph: What Catholic Tradition Teaches about the Man Who Raised God (El Cajon CA: Catholic Answers, 2021), p. 22.

The Holy Family immediately moved to Egypt and this dream most likely saved their lives, because after this Herod's army swept through the Bethlehem region and killed all the young boys.

Joseph had another dream when the family was in Egypt, when an angel informed him that it was safe to return to Nazareth:

> When Herod had died, behold, the angel of the Lord appeared in a dream to Joseph in Egypt and said, "Rise, take the child and his mother and go to the land of Israel, for those who sought the child's life are dead." He rose, took the child and his mother, and went to the land of Israel. But when he heard that Archelaus was ruling over Judea in place of his father Herod, he was afraid to go back there. And because he had been warned in a dream, he departed for the region of Galilee. He went and dwelt in a town called Nazareth, so that what had been spoken through the prophets might be fulfilled, "He shall be called a Nazorean." (Matt. 2:19-23, *NABRE*)

Joseph had a great relationship with angels!

Joseph's foundation in the Hebrew scriptures and customs in the Jewish community of Nazareth would have made him familiar with angels in the Old Testament. That might have made the visitations from angels less surprising, but what Joseph experienced had great power, enough to change his direction in life and protect Jesus and Mary.

Joseph then devoted his life to caring for Mary and Jesus, even though he and Mary had to move from place to place to protect Jesus, and themselves. He cared for the Holy Family all his life, and he taught Jesus about carpentry. Joseph loved his wife and his son, and he serves as a great example for us all.

How It Felt

The change Joseph experienced was a change from rejecting the supernatural circumstances of his life, to accepting that God had a directing hand in his circumstances. He came to believe that God was acting in his life and wanted him to participate in Jesus' upbringing in a particular way. Joseph resisted the change at first, and then through supernatural intervention, he came to accept it. Love for Mary also may have played a role in his acceptance, as seen by his devotion to her and the child and his original wish not to put her through any pain when she was found to be with child.

What You and I Can Do

From Joseph, you and I can learn to take our everyday circumstances seriously and be loving and responsible to those around us. We can also learn to pay attention to religious leaders, as well as to our inner thoughts and dreams, learning to recognize when God is talking to us. We can realize from Joseph's story that it's important to build a strong faith foundation in order for us to recognize when a communication or a dream is from God, and then to act on it.

Joseph did not hesitate – he took Mary into his home soon after he understood the message of the angel. From then on, when he had dreams from angels, he acted immediately, and we can take heart from Joseph's example. If we have a sense of what

God is asking us to do, we can take the message seriously, checking it against scripture and what we know about our Catholic faith, and asking knowledgeable others who can provide additional perspective.

St. Paul (c. 5 – c. 64/65 A.D.)

Who He Was

Saint Paul was first introduced to us in the New Testament as the person who was persecuting Christians. He supported the stoning of the first martyr, Stephen, by standing by the coats of those who threw the stones ("[Stephen] said, 'Behold, I see the heavens opened and the Son of Man standing at the right hand of God.' But they cried out in a loud voice, covered their ears, and rushed upon him together. They threw him out of the city, and began to stone him. The witnesses laid down their cloaks at the feet of a young man named Saul" (Acts 7:56-58 *NABRE*). Paul was called "Saul" at that time.

Paul was well educated as a devout Jew who observed religious customs and traditions. His teacher was a well-known Jewish scholar named Gamaliel. He recounted his story in Jerusalem to fellow Jews: "I am a Jew, born in Tarsus in Cilicia, but brought up in this city. At the feet of Gamaliel I was educated strictly in our ancestral law and was zealous for God, just as all of you are today" (Acts 22:3 *NABRE*).

How He Changed

During a trip to Damascus Paul encountered Jesus in a dramatic way. The biblical record describes him as falling to the ground and hearing the voice of Jesus. He was blinded for several days:

On that journey as I drew near to Damascus, about noon a great light from the sky suddenly shone around me. I fell to the ground and heard a voice saying to me, 'Saul, Saul, why are you persecuting me?' I replied, 'Who are you, sir?' And he said to me, 'I am Jesus the Nazorean whom you are persecuting.' My companions saw the light but did not hear the voice of the one who spoke to me. I asked, 'What shall I do, sir?' The Lord answered me, 'Get up and go into Damascus, and there you will be told about everything appointed for you to do.' Since I could see nothing because of the brightness of that light, I was led by hand by my companions and entered Damascus. (Acts 22:6-11, *NABRE*)

This was a dramatic conversion. Paul heard from Jesus directly, and Jesus identified himself by name. His whole world was turned upside down. He became a strong and devoted follower of Jesus, writing many letters which are now part of the New Testament and ultimately dying for his faith.

Paul's background provided a strong foundation for examining the legitimacy of Jesus as the Messiah and pointing out in his writings the reasons why the teachings of Jesus reflect with accuracy the sayings of the prophets and the fulfillment of the Mosaic law. Even though Paul was an expert in Jewish law, a vision from God directed him to preach to the Gentiles: "During [the] night Paul had a vision. A Macedonian stood before him and implored him with these words, 'Come over to Macedonia and help us'" (Acts 16:9 *NABRE*).

Not many of us have the intellect or the dedication to relentlessly defend our faith the way Paul did, first as a devout Jew and then as a devout Christian. Even in prison Paul wrote letters to the newly established Christian churches to explain the faith and keep them on the right track with a correct understanding of the mission of Jesus and how he fulfilled the Old Testament prophecies.

Paul's conversion was one to appreciate as a sudden change in his outlook. He revised his theological understanding of the scriptures and became a major author of the New Testament. From a tormentor of Christians, he became their leader and guide, showing them the way to understand Jesus and grow closer to him in faith.

Although Paul's initial conversion was sudden and dramatic, there were many incremental moments of change as he learned to treat all people as Christian brothers and sisters. For example, in his letter to Philemon Paul recognized the slave Onesimus as a brother in Christ, rather than as a slave, and he encouraged Philemon, his owner, also a brother in Christ, to treat him that way also (Philemon 1:7-22).

How It Felt

Paul must have felt disoriented and confused, shocked and stunned, after his first encounter with Jesus on the road to Damascus. Later, when he had time to process it, his entire life changed. He may not have felt like his old self. He was willing to die for his faith, and he went through significant times of suffering over and over again, from beatings to imprisonment to shipwreck. None of these deterred him from his faith in Jesus or his mission to spread the Gospel.

Paul's writings have a mystical quality about his union with Christ, speaking about Christ in him and he in Christ. According to John Tyson, "The heart of the Christian religion is union with Christ; union with Christ is both the means and the goal of Christian Spirituality."[1] Quoting James Stewart in *A Man in Christ: The Vital Element of St. Paul's Religion,* Tyson continues:

> Everything that religion meant for Paul is focused for us in such great words as these: 'I live yet not I, but Christ liveth in me' [Gal 2:20]. 'There is therefore now no condemnation to them which are in Christ Jesus' [Rom

---

[1] John R. Tyson, "Introduction," in *Invitation to Christian Spirituality: An Ecumenical Anthology,* ed. John R. Tyson (New York: Oxford University Press, 1999), p. 27.

8:1]. 'He that is joined unto the Lord is one spirit' [1 Cor 6:17].

What You and I Can Do

There are many blessings we can receive from St. Paul's conversion. From his understanding of union with Christ we realize that we are never alone when we are in Christ and Christ is in us. In fact, Paul couldn't get away from Jesus. We can be sure that God will find us because he wants us as his children. He can be very convincing, as Paul found out.

From Paul we can also learn to read scripture deeply and study the connections between the Old Testament and the New Testament. We can also be reminded that no effort to learn about God or connect with God in prayer is ever wasted. This points to the benefits of a good theological education.

Also we can take away Paul's intensity of spirit in his pursuit of God, both before and after his conversion. We can worship God without fear and he will guide our feet into the way of peace.[2]

---

[2] See Luke:1, Canticle of Zechariah.

St. Teresa of Avila (1515-1582)

Who She Was

St. Teresa of Jesus (Avila) was born in 1515 and entered the Carmelite Order in 1535. She died in 1582. During her life, she underwent a number of significant changes, including entering Carmel against the wishes of her father, becoming a leader in the reform of the Order, and founding many monasteries for women and men in Spain. She grew in her relationship with God through mystical experiences in prayer and service to God as a leader in the Carmelite Order. She wrote autobiographical and spiritual books to recount her experiences both in practical life and in her deep prayer life, in order to communicate her methods and practices to the nuns and friars of the reformed way of life which God led her to embrace and promote.

How She Changed

Shortly after Teresa entered religious life as a Carmelite nun, she experienced a very serious illness that left her bedridden for a long time. After she recovered, she had great difficulty with prayer: She wrote: "And very often, for some years, I was more anxious that the hour I had determined to spend in prayer be over than I was to remain there . . . and so unbearable was the sadness I felt on entering the oratory, that I had to muster up all my courage."[1]

Teresa had feelings of compunction and guilt over this, and she had difficulty in prayer for about eighteen years. "She didn't realize that the mind, or imagination, and feelings can wander, as St. John of the Cross points out, while the soul on a deeper level may remain quiet in a hardly perceptible contemplation." These feelings became more intense as she experienced more of God's "transcendent majesty, and of the shabbiness of sin beside His boundless outpouring love."[2] Her feelings of humiliation and lowliness preceded her experience of Gods majesty. As

---

[1] Kieran Kavanaugh, O.C.D., "The Book of Her Life – Introduction," *The Collected Works of St. Teresa of Avila*, Vol. 1, tr. Kieran Kavanaugh, O.C.D. and Otilio Rodriguez, O.C.D. (Washington DC: ICS Publications, 1987), p. 20.

[2] Kavanaugh, "Introduction," p. 21.

she realized this a conversion occurred: "Teresa began, then, at the time of this conversion, to experience passively and in a living way the presence of God in the center of her soul."[3]

Teresa reported another change in her spiritual life when she experienced a vision of herself in hell:

> A long time after the Lord had already granted me many of the favors I've mentioned and other very lofty ones, while I was in prayer one day, I suddenly found that, without knowing how, I had seemingly been put in hell. I understood that the Lord wanted me to see the place the devils had prepared there for me which I merited because of my sins ... I was left terrified, and still am now in writing about this almost six years later ... Since that time, as I say, everything seems to me easy when compared undergoing for a moment what I suffered there in hell.[4]

---

[3] Kavanaugh, "Introduction," p. 20.

[4] Teresa of Avila, The Book of Her Life, in *The Collected Works of St. Teresa of Avila,* Vol. 1, tr. Kieran

How It Felt

Teresa reported going from the inability to concentrate in prayer for many years, to accepting that God works in the soul even when the mind wanders. She was able to experience the depth of God's love after years of effort, and this was related to her humility and feelings of compunction. She wrote about her experiences in prayer in *The Way of Perfection* as a guide for her religious sisters, after she had come to understand the various degrees of prayer.

After her experience in hell, where she saw and felt the torments of what life in hell would be like for her, she reported still feeling terrified of the memory but that everything seemed easy compared to even a moment of the experience of hell. This was like a second conversion for her that led to a further deepening of her spiritual life.

Kavanaugh, O.C.D. and Otilio Rodriguez, O.C.D. (Washington DC: ICS Publications, 1987), ch. 32, 1-5.

What You and I Can Do

From Teresa we can learn to persevere in prayer, and not to worry about distractions even if they persist. We may at times feel sad about being far from God spiritually, but this should not lead to abandoning our prayers. Rather, keep going, and understand that God is working in the soul.

We can also take away the recognition that it's possible to write even in difficult circumstances and when we are very busy. This is true of other tasks as well. Teresa led a busy life of leadership, including the reform of the Carmelite Order, yet she found time to relate her experiences of prayer to others commit them to writing for the benefit of those she directed in the spiritual life.

St. Padre Pio (1887-1968)

Who He Was

St. Padre Pio was an Italian Franciscan friar who started a health center in Italy to alleviate suffering and treat the sick. He had mystical experiences from his childhood into adulthood, including fighting demons and being able to "locate" himself in multiple locations at the same time. Witnesses reported seeing him visit them when he was physically located in another part of the world. He reported an experience in January, 1905, of suddenly finding himself in another place while remaining in the choir during his studies at Sant'Elia a Pianisi:

> Several days ago, I had an extraordinary experience. Around 11:00 p.m. on January 18, 1905, Fra Anastasio and I were in the choir when suddenly I found myself far away in a wealthy home where the father was dying while a child was being born. Then the Most Blessed Virgin Mary appeared to me and said to me, "I am entrusting this child to you. Now

she is a diamond in the rough, but I want you to work with her, polish her, and make her as shining as possible, because one day I wish to adorn myself with her."[1]

In the book *Padre Pio: The True Story,* by C. Bernard Ruffin, the author goes into great depth describing Padre Pio's early life.

When he was eight, he witnessed the cure of a boy attributed to St. Pellegrino in a church near his home (pp. 31-2). One time, as a boy, he told his father where to dig to find water, because Jesus told him where to dig (p. 32). His mother took him to visit a hospital during World War I where he witnessed a soldier die, which left a strong impression on him (p. 32). When he was ten, he met a Capuchin friar, Fra Camillo, and from that moment he wanted to be "a friar with a beard" (p. 33).[2]

---

[1] C. Bernard Ruffin, *Padre Pio: The True Story,* (Huntington IN: Our Sunday Visitor, 2018), p. 62.

[2] Ruffin, *Padre Pio,* 2018.

Padre Pio is known for the *stigmata*, wounds in his hands that would not stop bleeding, reminiscent of the wounds in Jesus' hands when he was nailed to the cross. These wounds were spiritual in their cause but resulted in bleeding and pain for fifty years of Padre Pio's life. They were healed as mysteriously as they appeared, after Padre Pio was told that he would have them only for the prescribed amount of time.

Padre Pio also was known for seeing into the future or being aware of the state of loved ones who had died. Many people came to him for confession. It was as though Padre Pio understood the depth of their souls. He was merciful but he wanted people to be honest.

How He Changed

Padre Pio reported a visit from Jesus in a letter to his spiritual director Padre Benedicto de San Marco, on July 7, 1913:

> This morning after Mass while I was feeling quite troubled about this matter I was suddenly seized by a violent headache and there

and then it seemed to me impossible to continue my thanksgiving. This condition increased my torment. Moreover, a great aridity invaded my soul and who knows what might not have happened if what I am about to tell you had not taken place.

Our Lord appeared and spoke to me as follows: "My son, do not fail to write down what you hear today from my lips, so that you may not forget it. I am faithful and no creature will be lost unwittingly. Light is very different from darkness. I invariably attract to myself the soul to whom I am accustomed to speak. On the contrary, the wiles of the devil tend to separate it from me. I never inspire in the soul any fears which drive it away from me, the devil never places in the soul any fears which induce it to draw near to me."

"If the fears which the soul feels at certain moments of its life on the score of its eternal salvation proceed from me, they can be recognized by the peace and serenity they leave in the soul."

This vision and locution of Our Lord plunged my soul into such peace and happiness that all the sweetness of the world appears tasteless in comparison to even a single drop of this bliss. [3]

Visits from Jesus such as this show Padre Pio's closeness to Jesus. He received directives from Jesus which guided his life.

How It Felt

Padre Pio grew up in a Christian home. He was drawn to the Franciscans due to a Franciscan friar that visited Pietrielcina, his home town, when he was young. He entered a new stage of his spiritual journey at the time he received the *stigmata*, the wounds in his hands. This brought him under public scrutiny and led to times of humiliation. However, it also

---

[3] "Discerning the Voice of the Lord: Insights form Padre Pio's Testimony," September 11, 2023, https://capuchinswest.org/post-news/ discerning-the-voice-of-the-lord-insights-form-padre-pios-testimony/.

drew people to him for answers to their problems and for spiritual healing.

Padre Pio experienced visions and heard heavenly voices. "It would seem that from his study of Saint Teresa, Saint John of the Cross, and other mystical writers, Fra Pio learned to distinguish between three types of visions, the bodily, the imaginative, and the intellectual."[4]

Padre Pio grew closer to the Lord throughout his life, sometimes taking hours to celebrate Mass. He encouraged others to take time for prayer and worship, and to be honest in their confessions and prayers.

Perhaps the most dramatic experience in Padre Pio's spiritual life was the receiving of the wounds in his hands, the *stigmata*. He was deeply affected by this change as it brought him public attention but also launched him into a role of popularity which brought people to him and to the Lord through him for their spiritual healing and growth.

On September 17, 1918, Padre Pio offered himself as a victim for the boys of the "Seraphic College,"

---

[4] Ruffin, *Padre Pio,* 2018, p. 57.

where he was principal ... The Spanish influenza epidemic was present in the college and almost all of the boys were ill. Several days later they noticed that Padre Pio kept his hands covered and they could sometimes see the red spots on his hands. Nina Campanile recalled later that "when she handed him a Mass offering, she noticed a mark on his right hand and commented, 'Oh, Father, you've burned your hand!' He turned pale and hid his hand in his habit ... Padre Pio exclaimed, 'If you only knew the humiliation this causes me.'"[5]

Padre Pio had repeated experiences with demons. He had continual bleeding from the *stigmata* for fifty years. He had repeated experiences of bilocation. His ministry remained public with times of intense private prayer, sometimes battling demons all night.

Padre Pio sometimes complained of the challenges associated with religious superiors and detractors who expressed doubts about the *stigmata's* authenticity. He was repeatedly examined by doctors and challenged by brothers and others who devalued

---

[5] Ruffin, *Padre Pio,* 2018, p. 139.

him. He must have felt distressed, discouraged and rejected at times. At other times he was so close to God, especially during Mass, that he likely felt encouraged internally and strengthened for what he had to endure at the hands of doctors and naysayers.

What remained always with him was Padre Pio's faith in God. He was known for his advice to pray always, and not worry. God would take care of everything, and we should trust Him.

Padre Pio also loved his family and cared for people. He had an inner circle of close friends and supporters to whom he could go for encouragement and friendship.

What You and I Can Do

We can learn from the life of Padre Pio to worry less and trust God more. His faithfulness throughout many trials can help us cope with painful experiences we may go through, particularly if our Catholic beliefs are challenged by coworkers or family members. We can stay strong in the midst of trials and pray to Padre Pio for encouragement and help.

We can also benefit by remembering Padre Pio's *stigmata* as signs from God of his faith and of God's choosing him for special work. God has chosen us, too, for special work. We are called to rise to the challenge and serve God even when the going gets rough, and we can be inspired by Padre Pio's perseverance to continue the effort, no matter what.

Brother Lawrence of the Resurrection (1614-1691)

Who He Was

Brother Lawrence began his life as Nicholas Hermann. He was born in 1614 at Hériménil in the Lorraine area of northeastern France. At age eighteen, "a sudden, cosmic intuition of the grandeur and presence of God grasped him profoundly . . . It was a silent call of the divine mystery and a first conversion."[1]

Later in life Br. Lawrence told the story of his conversion to Fr. Joseph de Beaufort, a Parisian priest, who wrote it down: "One day in winter while he was looking at a tree stripped of its leaves, and he realized that in a little while its leaves would reappear, followed by its flowers and fruit, he received a profound insight into God's providence that has never been erased from his soul. This insight

---

[1] Brother Lawrence of the Resurrection, *The Practice of the Presence of God,* ed. Conrad De Meester, O.C.D., tr. Salvatore Sciurba, O.C.D. (Washington DC: ICS Publications, 1994), p. xviii.

completely freed him from the world, and gave him such a love for God that he could not say it had increased during the more than forty years that had passed."[2]

How He Changed

This stunning conversion lasted Br. Lawrence all his life – it was not a passing realization, but it launched him into a practice he would use throughout his life, what he would call the practice of the presence of God.

Despite his profound early experience of God's providence as seen in nature, Brother Lawrence did not change all at once. Shortly after this experience he joined the military, but he returned to his father's house after he was wounded. When he was twenty-six, he joined the Order of the Discalced Carmelites in Paris as a lay brother through the influence of his uncle:[3]

---

[2] Brother Lawrence, The Practice of the Presence of God, p. 89.

[3] Brother Lawrence, The Practice of the Presence of God, pp. xviii-xvix.

He often relived the perils of his military service, the vanity and corruption of the times, the instability of other people, the treason of an enemy, and the infidelity of his friends. It was only after intense reflection, inner struggles, sighs, and tears that, overcome by the power of eternal truths, he firmly resolved to devote himself to the practice of the Gospel and to follow in the footsteps of his uncle, a holy Discalced Carmelite.[4]

During his early years as a Carmelite, disturbing thoughts and memories plagued Brother Lawrence and he could not find peace. Finally, he had a realization that provided a breakthrough:

> One day, he was reflecting on the sufferings that afflicted his soul, and knowing that it was for the love of God and for fear of displeasing him that he was enduring them, he made a firm resolution to bear them, not only for the rest of his life, but even for all eternity if it

---

[4] Brother Lawrence, The Practice of the Presence of God, p. 7.

pleased God to so ordain it. 'It doesn't matter what I do or what I suffer so long as I remain lovingly united to his will in all things,' he said.[5]

Once he came to this conclusion and resolved to accept these sufferings, he experienced great peace and calm and "I found myself changed all at once. And my soul, until that time always in turmoil, experienced a deep inner peace as if it had found its center and place of rest."[6]

How It Felt

The method Brother Lawrence used to stay close to God was not found in books. After searching several books Brother Lawrence felt that these practices would burden him rather than "facilitate what I wanted and what I sought, namely, a means of being completely disposed to God. This led me to resolve

---

[5] Brother Lawrence, The Practice of the Presence of God, p. 11.

[6] Brother Lawrence, The Practice of the Presence of God, p. 53.

to give all for all. Thus, after offering myself entirely to God in atonement for my sins, I renounced for the sake of his love everything other than God, and I began to live as if only he and I existed in the world."

Brother Lawrence turned to God in his daily activities as well as during his times of mental prayer: "At every moment, all the time, in the most intense periods of my work I banished and rid from my mind everything that was capable of taking the thought of God away from me" [7] He wrote that the practice of the presence of God "consists in taking delight in and becoming accustomed to his divine company, speaking humbly and conversing lovingly with him all the time, at every moment, without rule or measure, especially in times of temptation, suffering, aridity, [and] weariness," and these brief conversations should come "from the purity and simplicity of our hearts."[8]

From these accounts we may see that Brother Lawrence had two major conversions, the first when

---

[7] Brother Lawrence, The Practice of the Presence of God, p. 75.

[8] Brother Lawrence, The Practice of the Presence of God, p. 105.

he contemplated the goodness of God in nature as he pondered how God would bring life back to a tree after a long winter, and the second after wrestling with disturbing thoughts and memories and resolving to bear this anxiety forever if God so willed it, realizing that nothing could take him away from God's presence.

After the first conversion Brother Lawrence continued in the secular world for a time, but he ultimately joined the Carmelites, where he worked as a lay brother in the kitchen. His spiritual growth as a Carmelite led him to develop a practice of always keeping an awareness of God's presence in all his daily activities. Even so, he was tormented by distractions and memories which disturbed his peace of mind, but once he accepted this he was changed again, realizing that nothing could separate him from the love of God.

What You and I Can Do

From Brother Lawrence we can find encouragement during prayer, when our minds wander. We simply bring them back to God. We can also feel encouraged when we do not find books helpful – Brother Lawrence trusted how God was leading him and felt free to develop his own method of remaining close to God and appreciating the enjoyable conversations he had with God.

I find hope in Brother Lawrence when I reflect on how he found help in his community while also relying on God alone, offering "all for all." God gives me grace for the day and company for the night, and he is there whenever I check. There is not a time that I remember to notice God, that he is not there. Brother Lawrence lived this awareness to a maximum level. I find this inspiring.

Another part of Brother Lawrence's life that can help us is how he let go of the past. He ultimately came to terms with accepting that he would always be influenced by his past. This freed him from trying to defend against it. That freedom drew him even closer to God. The same can be true for us.

St. Mother Teresa of Calcutta (1910-1997)

Who She Was

Saint Mother Teresa of Calcutta (1910-1997) was the founder of the Missionaries of Charity and the winner of the Nobel Peace Prize for her work with the poor in India and throughout the world. After growing up in Albania, she joined the Sisters of Loreto and moved to Calcutta to teach history and geography. From there she heard a call from God to work with the poorest of the poor, and she formed a new religious order called the Missionaries of Charity. This organization has established many houses of prayer and services to the poor in countries around the world.

Mother Teresa experienced her first call to the religious life in Albania, when she was at home with her mother and sister. Her father had died when she was eight years old. "By the age of twelve Agnes felt herself called to the religious life, an intensely personal experience on which she would not elaborate . . . 'It is a private matter. It was not a vision.'"[1] Agnes (Mother Teresa's given name) joined the Loreto Sisters in 1928. She had grown up in a devout Catholic family and attended the local church regularly.

After a brief novitiate with the Sisters of Loreto in Ireland, Mother Teresa sailed to Calcutta, India in 1929 to teach at a Catholic girls' high school. She taught history and geography, which prepared her for later work establishing houses for the Missionaries of Charity, a religious order she would later establish throughout the world. She had a good understanding of many countries and what their needs were.[2]

What She Did

Every Sunday Mother Teresa visited the slums in Calcutta and brought what she could find in the donations received at the school, which no one else wanted, to the people she met. Teresa remained at the school in Calcutta even during the war years

---

[1] Kathryn Spink, *Mother Teresa: An Authorized Biography* (New York: HarperCollins, 2011), p. 6.

[2] Spink, *Mother Teresa*, pp. 12-16.

when conditions deteriorated in and around her school. During this period she was appointed headmistress.[3]

In 1946 Mother Teresa was exhausted and she became ill. Since she was so weak, she was directed to "go on retreat to the hill station of Darjeeling. The intention was that in the interests of her health she should undergo a period of spiritual renewal and a physical break from the work. Instead, as it transpired, she was to be called to another form of work and service within the religious life she had already chosen."[4]

This led to Mother Teresa receiving the "call within a call" to help the poorest of the poor:

> On September 10, 1946, a date now celebrated annually by Missionaries of Charity . . . as "Inspiration Day," on the rattling, dusty train journey to Darjeeling, came what Mother Teresa would subsequently describe as "the call within a call." . . . "The call of God to be a Missionary of Charity," she once

---

[3] Spink, *Mother Teresa,* pp. 17-20.

[4] Spink, *Mother Teresa,* p. 22.

confided, "is the hidden treasure for me, for which I have sold all to purchase it . . . This is what I want to do for God . . . I was to leave the convent and help the poor while living among them. It was an order. To fail it would have been to break the faith."[5]

This call was a powerful directive to leave the Sisters of Loreto and establish the Missionaries of Charity, whose main work would be serving the very poor throughout the world. She established homes for the dying, to take in people from the streets who had no one to care for them as they lay dying in the poorest sections of town. In addition to their active work, Mother Teresa also established houses of contemplative prayer in which members of the Missionaries of Charity would pray for the active work of the apostolate. Prayer and activity were both important aspects of Mother Teresa's personal life, missionary life, and corporate life in the new order she established.

---

[5] Spink, *Mother Teresa,* p. 22.

Mother Teresa heard God's call in her first experience of a major vocational shift, in Albania, when God called her to become a religious sister and join the Sisters of Loreto. She heard Jesus when she was on the train to Darjeeling years later, asking her to serve the poorest of the poor in India. This was the call within a call.

Mother Teresa recognized the light of God in the people she served. She saw Jesus in the poor people who came to her. She taught her nuns to practice living the gospel in five words: "You did it unto me." This referred to the following Bible passage:

> "For I was hungry and you gave me food, I was thirsty and you gave me drink, a stranger and you welcomed me, naked and you clothed me, ill and you cared for me, in prison and you visited me." Then the righteous will answer him and say, "Lord, when did we see you hungry and feed you, or thirsty and give you drink? When did we see you a stranger and welcome you, or naked and clothe you? When did we see you ill or in prison, and visit you?" And the king will say

to them in reply, "Amen, I say to you, whatever you did for one of these least brothers of mine, you did for me." (Matt 25:35-40, *NABRE*)

Mother Teresa's first conversion, her call to religious life, was interior, rooted in prayer and visiting the Blessed Sacrament in her home town. It was not pleasant for her mother to lose her in this way, especially since she left home after her father died. Her mother could have used the help. But it was a powerful call and one that could not be ignored.

Mother Teresa's second conversion, her call to serve the poorest of the poor, was also rooted in prayer, this time on the train on her way to her personal retreat. She had a close relationship with Jesus even though it did not seem like it at times.[6] She operated in faith, believing in the strength of the instruction she received and confirming it in scripture.

---

[6] See Mother Teresa, *Come Be My Light – The Private Writings of the Saint of Calcutta,* ed. Brian Kolodiejchuk, M.C. (New York: Doubleday, 2007).

How It Felt

Mother Teresa experienced growth in the religious life through her teaching and observing conditions in Calcutta. As she reflected on the plight of her neighbors, the context was established to promote the call Jesus wanted her to hear from him, to serve the very people for whom she had already developed a heart.

Mother Teresa's major changes were dramatic, but were prepared for through prayer and the support of her immediate family and the Sisters of Loreto. The changes were dramatic each time, but one can see the build-up of her spiritual growth that fostered the apparently sudden shift in direction each time.

What was repeated in Mother Teresa's life were her devotion to prayer and her willingness to obey God. Also we see her simplicity in how she communicated and distilled the gospel to her sisters in religious life. She kept things simple and pure, keeping in mind that God was present in every human being. She was relentless in pursuing her vision of houses to serve the poor in many jurisdictions throughout the world.

Mother Teresa felt tired at times, due to her long hours of work each day. She also felt fulfilled seeing the progress in her work and the help she and her sisters were able to give many people. It must have been gratifying when some of her former students so happily joined her in her new venture when she left the school to serve the poor. Her letters, published after her death, described aridity in her spiritual life. At times she felt lonely and frustrated, not hearing from God after she had changed her whole life in obedience to the will of God as she understood it.

Mother Teresa persevered in her mission and kept the faith even when it felt dark and confusing. She knew what Jesus had told her, and she understood this was consistent with his directives in scripture. She could trust him, and she worked with a spiritual director who believed in her inner experiences and outward actions to live out the mission God had given her. Mother Teresa's faith stayed strong and was continuously nourished by prayer. She encouraged her nuns to start their days with prayer and to pray longer on busy days.

What You and I Can Do

We can learn from Mother Teresa to pray often, and to trust what we hear in prayer. We can appreciate her dedicated single-mindedness to follow Jesus in the face of many obstacles. We can also adopt her large vision, global in its scope, to apply our calling world-wide. With Jesus we can do what seems impossible. Mother Teresa embodied that idea, relying on him to pave the way for houses in numerous countries.

We can also take away the idea of compassion from Mother Teresa. She had compassion for people from all walks of life and all cultures. She did not sugar-coat reality. She faced difficult situations with God's strength and great determination.

We may be inspired by Mother Teresa to persevere in strength, humility and dedication to whatever God has called us to do, even if it means a change in location, direction or purpose. We must persevere with what we know he has asked us for, even if it seems dark or difficult at times. Mother Teresa, pray for us!

St. Augustine of Hippo (354-430)

Who He Was

Saint Augustine was a prolific writer, theologian and philosopher of the 4th century. He was Bishop of Hippo in north Africa, and he also lived in Milan where he was influenced by St. Ambrose, the Bishop there. Augustine died in 430 AD.

St. Augustine grew up with a Christian mother and pagan father who eventually came to Christ late in life. His mother prayed for Augustine constantly, and even followed him to Italy when he went to study rhetoric there. Augustine was a gifted orator.

Augustine is most well-known for his book, *Confessions,* which is about his own spiritual journey, his approach to God and his repentance from sin:

> We read here [in the *Confessions*] about the human soul's longing for God, as well as the wantonness of human sin. We read about the significance of Christian conversion, and we learn of the providence of God that (unbeknownst to himself) wooed Augustine to

return to the Father's household. The way "home" to God is marked out by confession. The word *confession* (Lat. *confessio*), as Augustine applied it, meant the 'accusation of oneself and the praise of God.' Hence, the book assumes the form of an extended prayer or conversation with God. In this way, then, *Confessions* is not merely a record of Augustine's pilgrimage, it is the medicine of his own healing and perhaps that of his readers as well.[1]

How He Changed

Augustine's conversion seemed dramatic, but he prepared for it by wrestling with himself:

> When I was trying to reach a decision about serving the Lord my God, as I had long intended to do, it was I who willed to take this course and again it was I who willed not to take it. It was I and I alone. But I neither

---

[1] Tyson, Invitation to Christian Spirituality, p. 104.

willed to do it nor refused to do it with my full will. So I was at odds with myself.[2]

This was during a time that he was restless in his own soul and pondering Christian concepts which he had read in scripture and heard in Church, especially from St. Ambrose.

Augustine recorded the dramatic moment by describing the state of his soul:

> I was in torment, reproaching myself more bitterly than ever as I twisted and turned in my chain ... And you, O Lord, never ceased to watch over my secret heart. In your stern mercy you lashed me with the twin scourge of fear and shame ... In my heart I kept saying "Let it be now, let it be now!," and merely by saying this I was on the point of making the resolution. I was on the point of making it, but I did not succeed ... My lower instincts, which had taken firm hold of me, were

---

[2] Augustine, *Confessions,* tr. R. S. Pine-Coffin (London: Penguin Books, 1961), p. 173.

stronger than the higher, which were untried.[3]

Augustine's interior battles were not only intellectual – his feelings broke out in a powerful episode of crying. Eventually he had a breakthrough:

> I probed the hidden depths of my soul and wrung its pitiful secrets from it, and when I mustered them all before the eyes of my heart, a great storm broke within me, bringing with it a great deluge of tears. I stood up and left Alypius so that I might weep and cry to my heart's content . . . I felt that I was still the captive of my sins, and in my misery I kept crying "How long shall I go on saying 'tomorrow, tomorrow'? Why not now? Why not make an end of my ugly sins at this moment?"
>
> I was asking myself these questions, weeping all the while with the most bitter sorrow in my heart, when all at once I heard the

---

[3] Augustine, *Confessions,* p. 175.

sing-song voice of a child in a nearby house . . . again and again it repeated the refrain, "Take it and read, take it and read." . . . So I hurried back to the place where Alypius was sitting, for when I stood up to move away I had put down the book containing Paul's Epistles. I seized it and opened it, and in silence I read the first passage on which my eyes fell: *Not in revelling and drunkenness, not in lust and wantonness, not in quarrels and rivalries. Rather, arm yourselves with the Lord Jesus Christ; spend no more thought on nature and nature's appetites* [Romans 13:13-14]. I had no wish to read more and no need to do so. For in an instant as I came to the end of the sentence, it was as though the light of confidence flooded into my heart and all the darkness of doubt was dispelled.[4]

Augustine understood clearly that this scripture passage should apply to him, and he changed his life after this. He believed in Jesus, much to his mother's

---

[4] Augustine, *Confessions,* pp. 177-178.

delight. He turned his life around and became one of the greatest theologians the world has ever known.

How It Felt

St. Augustine encountered Jesus in the scriptures and through the testimony of his friend and spiritual guide, St. Ambrose. When Augustine heard, "Take and read," he responded with obedience. Augustine also applied his mind in his search for truth. He needed intellectual reasons to consider Christ's teachings, and with Ambrose as guide his agile mind was put on the right path. This paved the way for his emotional and spiritual conversion in the garden. His mother also pleaded to God constantly for him.

The nature of the change for Augustine was intellectual, emotional and in the activities of his daily life. He left his common-law wife but stayed connected with his son, Adeodatus. He applied his formidable mental powers in service of the Lord and seeking Christian truth. His writings show that he was dedicated in spreading the Christian message, and his *Confessions* recounts the story of his own conversion. His mind, heart, and actions changed to conform to the teachings and inspirations of Christ.

There were incremental shifts in Augustine's conversion. His regular meetings with Ambrose gradually educated him in the gospel message, the letters of St. Paul and other scripture. This led him to think about Jesus and his role in salvation. Augustine also was a deeply questioning person. He had been involved with Manicheism, a philosophical system about dualities such as darkness and light, and matter and spirit, prior to Christianity. He was seeking truth but did not find the fullness of Truth until he encountered Jesus and had the Christian message explained to him.

The prayers and influence of his mother, the intellectual inspiration of Ambrose, his own suffering and remorse over his sinfulness, and the sudden mystical encounter in the garden with its corresponding scriptural impact all contributed to Augustine's conversion. The most dramatic part of Augustine's conversion occurred when he heard the children's voices in his garden telling him to take and read something, then he went inside and read the scripture in Romans that said not to make any provision for the flesh.

Before Augustine's conversion he felt out of balance and uncomfortable. He could no longer accept the Manichean system of duality, but he could not yet accept Ambrose's presentation of the Christian view. Once Augustine accepted that Jesus was real and the Christian message was true, he must have felt relieved but chagrined at how many changes he had to make in his moral choices and lifestyle. I wonder if he also felt humbled since he had hung onto the wrong system for so long.

However, he made the necessary changes, and he was then able to wholeheartedly embrace Christ and his new calling to serve God. Later as the Bishop of Hippo, he would have to call on Christ for the power and resolve to defend the Christian faith during a time of controversy. Augustine's brilliant intellect and dedicated faith helped sort out these complex issues, and his willingness to document his views in writing has helped maintain the reasoning that has guided subsequent Church councils, theologians, philosophers and generations of believers for centuries.

What You and I Can Do

From St. Augustine we can identify several important takeaways. First, he was honestly seeking the truth about himself and about the world. He made many mistakes and he recognized his own lack of wholeheartedness and sincerity in his search. We can appreciate his gift of perspective and how he applied this to his life and to his spiritual goals.

Not many people are as honest as Augustine about their own sins. I would not recommend sharing our sins publicly, but within our hearts, with a confessor, and in prayer we can be open with God in all the depths of our heart.

We can also take away the help that friends such as Alypius, teachers such as St. Ambrose, and activities such as writing can provide. Augustine's writing helps us, and it may have helped him sort out his own inner life.

Finally, we can remember how helpful reading scripture can be in times of trial. Great breakthroughs often come after a time of depression and serious soul-searching. In that process, scripture can provide an anchor as it did for Augustine.

St. Ignatius of Loyola (1491-1556)

Who He Was

Iñigo Lopez de Recalde was from the Guipuzcoa province in a mountainous region of northern Spain. His parents were nobles and lived in the family castle in a time of knighthood and chivalry. During a battle against the French, Iñigo was wounded in his leg and underwent a long recovery. During this time he reflected on his inner life, his own life goals, and his past life. This resulted in a major conversion after which he devoted his life to serving God.[1]

During his recovery, Iñigo read books about the saints and the life of Christ. These readings inspired him to begin to change his life to detach from the things of the world, including possessions and social status, and seek a life of serving God. He noticed that his interior feelings when reading inspiring stories about the saints affected him differently from reading stories of chivalry and thinking worldly thoughts.

---

[1] Tyson, Invitation to Christian Spirituality, pp. 244-245.

He recorded his experience in his autobiography, which is written in the third person:

> As he was much given to reading worldly books of fiction, commonly labeled chivalry, when he felt better he asked to be given some of them to pass the time. But in that house none of those that he usually read could be found, so they gave him a life of Christ and a book of the lives of the saints in Castilian.
>
> As he read them over many times, he became rather fond of what he found written there ... In reading the life of Our Lord and of the saints, he stopped to think, reasoning within himself, "What if I should do what St. Francis did, and what St. Dominic did?" Thus he pondered over many things that he found good.[2]

---

[2] Ignatius of Loyola, *Spiritual Exercises and Selected Works,* ed. George E. Ganss, S. J. (New York: Paulist Press, 1991), p. 70.

What He Did

These musings not only led Ignatius (Iñigo) to consider how he might live his life in the future, but also they established the foundation for his spiritual exercises of discernment based on interior consolation and desolation. From his autobiography:

> The succession of such diverse thoughts lasted for quite some time, and he always dwelt at length on the thought that turned up, either of the worldly exploits he wished to perform or of these others of God that came to his imagination, until he tired of it and put it aside and turned to other matters.
>
> Yet there was this difference. When he was thinking of those things of the world he took much delight in them, but afterwards, when he was tired and put them aside, he found himself dry and dissatisfied. But when he thought of going to Jerusalem barefoot, and of eating nothing but plain vegetables and of practicing all the other rigors that he saw in the saints, not only was he consoled

when he had these thoughts, but even after putting them aside he remained satisfied and joyful.[3]

The time Ignatius took to ponder his readings and his thoughts helped him not only in his own conversion of heart, but it showed him how to guide others by helping them to become aware of their own interior "consolations" (good thoughts with lasting satisfaction, serving the Lord) and "desolations" (worldly thoughts without lasting satisfaction). This would become the basis of his spiritual exercises.

Ignatius completed his education in Paris and went on to establish the Company of Jesus (Jesuits). The Jesuits have become known as learned priests who serve the wishes of the Pope anywhere in the world. Ignatius is known for his spiritual exercises, long retreats, and rules of discernment, where we are guided by interior movements of the spirit including consolation and desolation. These practices can help us make significant decisions in our lives. The Jesuits

---

[3] Ignatius of Loyola, *Spiritual Exercises*, p. 71.

are also known for seeing God in all things, and doing everything for the glory of God.

How It Felt

Ignatius' prayer life was intense, especially during his conversion. Ignatius wanted freedom from his sins in his previous way of life, that of a soldier, as well as his involvement with women and drink. Before his conversion Ignatius had sought to rise in his noble standing in the Loyola household, but afterward he was seeking union with God.

Ignatius' focus was interior, communicating with Jesus through discernment of his own emotions or interior sense of God's will. This wasn't necessarily verbal. Rather, he discerned movements of the spirit within himself and interpreted these as signs from God.

Ignatius was sensitive to communications from God. He named his community the Company of Jesus which shows his devotion to Jesus. Ignatius wrote down the rules for discernment of spirits and guidance for others to develop their spiritual capacity to hear from God or be guided by God through interior awareness.

Ignatius' most intense change occurred after his recovery from the cannonball wound to his leg, when he left the Loyola estate and sought solitude with God in a cave at Manresa. He wrestled with God interiorly about his sins and about how to move forward. His entire value system changed as a result, leaving behind the affluent life of a nobleman for the poor life of a member of a community whose only focus was to serve God and the Church, and to teach others how to find God in everyday life and in their hearts.

Ignatius' conversion was launched through an injury that left him bedridden. Reading was important for his transition, because where he formerly would have read books about knighthood in a secular sense, now he turned to the "knights of God," the saints, and became inspired by their lives. The two books that most influenced him were *The Golden Legend* by a Dominican, Jacobo de Voragine, and the *Vita Christi*, by "the Carthusian," Ludolf of Saxony, a Carthusian monk who was formerly a Dominican. The *Vita Christi*, "Life of Christ," contained excerpts by well-known theologians on the full span of the life of Jesus Christ, including Ambrose, Bede, and others.

Ignatius' conversion was prepared for by his reading which occurred throughout a long convalescence to recover from a war injury. This part of the preparation was gradual and allowed him to slowly absorb knowledge about Jesus and his role in salvation history, as well as how the Catholic faith and understanding are lived out in the lives of many saints.

Ignatius underwent a dramatic conversion after he struck out on his own and wrestled with his interior leanings of the spirit. He emerged from this soul-searching period of isolation and prayer with great devotion to God and a way forward in his ability to form a group of followers to promote adherence to Christ and the Church.

For Ignatius, what was repeated was his reliance on his intelligence and introspective analysis of his own interior life. He was a thoughtful military leader and member of his family, recognizing his role in the nobility, before his conversion. Afterward, his sensitivity and analytical nature allowed him to document his conversion and prepare others for similar spiritual growth.

Ignatius went through a painful conversion process. He faced his sins. He was isolated with limited spiritual support, and he had to work out his suffering before God alone. Once Ignatius knew the direction his life should take, he went to Paris to study among students much younger than he was. He must have felt out of place, especially after leaving his life of nobility and rank. Still, he persevered and undoubtedly experienced humility during this time of intellectual growth.

Ignatius might have felt unsure and afraid as he launched out on his new direction in the formation of the Company of Jesus. His writings were examined by the Inquisition and that could have resulted in death. Ignatius was brave, both as a warrior in the military and as a warrior for God.

Ignatius trusted his mind and his ability to figure things out. He applied his reason to his faith and to situation in life. He knew he was called both to examine his own interior life intensely and to teach others how to do this. Both of these activities called for analysis and planning, and Ignatius applied the skills he developed as a military leader to his life of prayer and service to God.

What You and I Can Do

We can learn much from Ignatius. Interiorly, we can respect our inner spiritual experiences and learn to recognize which are the "good spirits" from God and which interior spiritual impulses are leading us away from God. We can also trust our intuition when we are called away to spend private time with God alone. God may need us to be away from the world and our own ambition for a while, in order to get through to us.

Finally, we can take courage from Ignatius' story. He was brave in battle and in the business of creating an entire religious order. Our organizational skills may be put to good use for God if we can hear his voice and trust our interior capacity to communicate with him.

St. Francis of Assisi (1181-1226)

Who He Was

Saint Francis of Assisi was born into a merchant family. His father was a textile merchant in Assisi, Italy. As a young man, Francis lived a carefree life among friends. He wrote songs and was known as a troubadour. His life changed after he rode into battle as a knight and returned to Assisi after he had been unsuccessful. He went through a conversion experience at a small church in San Damiano where he heard the Lord speaking to him to rebuild his Church. Francis collected stones from the village to rebuild church buildings but realized later that he was called to rebuild the Church spiritually.

Francis established the Order of Friars Minor (Franciscans) who are known for their emphasis on poverty and simplicity in charity and brotherhood. The women's branch of the Franciscans was founded by Francis' friend, the young noblewoman St. Clare, who established the Poor Clares in poverty under Francis' guidance. St. Clare is known for her devotion to poverty and to Jesus in the Eucharist.

How He Changed

While praying before a crucifix in the San Damiano church, Francis experienced Jesus telling him to rebuild his Church. He was walking by the church of San Damiano which was in disrepair, and he went inside to pray. "Prostrate before an image of the Crucified, he was filled with no little consolation as he prayed. While his tear-filled eyes were gazing at the Lord's cross, he heard with his bodily ears a voice coming from the cross, telling him three times: 'Francis, go and repair my house, which you see, is falling completely into ruin.'"[1]

This was a powerful motivation for Francis who got to work immediately:

> In 1207 St. Francis experienced a conversion and call to Christian service that radically altered the course of his life. In response to the call of Christ and in reaction to the decadence of his day, Francis embraced apostolic poverty and a mendicant life-style as the most

---

[1] Tyson, Invitation to Christian Spirituality, quoting Bonaventure, p. 162.

obvious way to imitate Christ and proclaim the Kingdom of God. Gradually a group of men embraced St. Francis's way of life and lived in community together.[2]

St. Francis' primary encounters with Jesus were through hearing, but he also was the first known person to experience the *stigmata,* the wounds of Christ in his own body. This occurred during prayer on a mountain, when an angel appeared to Francis and he was wounded in his hands, feet and side, in solidarity and connection with the wounds of Jesus on the cross:

> St. Francis saw above him, filling the whole heavens, some vast immemorial unthinkable power, ancient like the Ancient of Days, whose calm men had conceived under the forms of winged bulls or monstrous cherubim, and all that winged wonder was in pain like a wounded bird. This seraphic suffering, it is said, pierced his soul with a sword of grief

---

[2] Tyson, Invitation to Christian Spirituality, p. 163.

and pity; it may be inferred that some sort of mounting agony accompanied the ecstasy. Finally after some fashion the apocalypse faded from the sky and the agony within subsided; and silence and the natural air filled the morning twilight and settled slowly in the purple chasms and cleft abysses of the Apennines.

The head of the solitary sank, amid all that relaxation and quiet in which time can drift by with the sense of something ended and complete; and as he stared downwards, he saw the marks of nails in his own hands.[3]

Francis' prayer life was deep and focused on Christ. His spiritual program was one of simplicity and poverty. He had learned firsthand how the love of money can be distracting from the love of Christ. He wanted his followers to maintain this emphasis on poverty in order to maintain detachment from the world and focus on the things of God.

---

[3] G. K. Chesterton, *Saint Francis of Assisi* (New York: Doubleday, 2001), p. 121-122.

How It Felt

The nature of the spiritual change in Francis was prepared for by his disappointment in knightly pursuits. He turned back from what could have been a reputation-building escapade into battle, and he was called by God to engage in a different kind of battle. He was to detach from worldly pursuits and devote himself solely to God.

Francis recovered from his loss of reputation and disapproval by his father and emerged in rebellion against his father's way of life as a successful cloth merchant. His mother was more gentle but his father was harsh and wanted his son to follow in his footsteps.

At one point Francis removed his clothes and handed them back to his father publicly. He was seeking refuge in the Church and the Bishop was present, who draped Francis with a robe and accepted him and his choice to get out from under his father's powerful influence.

The other most dramatic event in Francis' conversion was his receiving of the *stigmata*. He is the first known person to be so in tune with the sufferings of Christ that these wounds mysteriously appeared on his body.

One thing that was repeated in Francis' life and conversion was his ability to draw people to himself, both as a troubadour and later as the founder and leader of the Franciscans. Francis repeatedly thought for himself on important matters, and contemplated his next moves in life in a thoughtful and introspective manner. Francis was open to women and respected his mother and his friend, Clare.

Life must have felt lonely to Francis after leaving his father's house, and even before, as he launched into a less secure lifestyle of poverty and detachment from the world. He must have worried at times about where the next meal was coming from or where the brothers would sleep. His faith carried him through these rough times and he relied on God to provide for his needs.

Francis had an element of service to God and others throughout his life. He was able to be alone, but he also sought the company of others. Francis had a strong devotion to his cause and to his activities. He was creative in his singing and in his launching out in a new direction that even required traveling to

Rome to get permission to found an order in radical poverty. He was creative and ambitious in his creation and development of the Order of Friars Minor.

What You and I Can Do

From Francis we can learn simplicity, reliance on God and detachment from worldly things. We can also see that it is possible to be so connected to Christ in prayer that we can hear him speak to us and empathize with his suffering on the cross. We may not experience Christ in exactly the same way Francis did, but we can be confident that Jesus will let us know what direction to go when the time comes.

St. Antony of the Desert (251-356)

Who He Was

A large part of what we know about St. Antony of the Desert we learn from the *Life of Antony*, by St. Athanasius of Alexandria (c. 296-373). Athanasius had great respect for Antony, and he wrote a biography of the saint's life that describes his conversion as a young man after his parents' death and how he lived a solitary, monastic life until he died at age 105.

Saint Antony is considered the father of monasticism. He lost his parents at a young age and was left taking care of his sister. He lived in Egypt in the 4th century. One day as he was hearing a gospel passage read he was inspired to leave all of his belongings and seek God wholeheartedly:

> Now it was not six months after the death of his parents, and going according to custom into the Lord's House, he communed with himself and reflected as he walked how the apostles [Mt 4:30] left everything and followed the Saviour; and how they in the Acts

[4:35] sold their possessions and brought [the proceeds] and laid them at the apostles' feet for distribution to the poor, and what a great hope was laid up for [such people] in heaven. Pondering over these things he entered the church, and as the Gospel was being read, and he heard the Lord saying to the rich man, "If you would be perfect, go and sell what you possess and give to the poor, and you will have treasure in heaven; and come, follow me" [Mt 19:21]. [To Antony it was] as though God had put him in mind of the saints, and [that] the passage had been read on his account, [he] went out ... from the church and gave the possessions of his forefather to the villagers ... And all the rest that was movable he sold, and having got together much money he gave it to the poor, reserving a little, however, for his sister's sake.[1]

Antony experienced a significant conversion that caused a change in his life. However, this conversion

---

[1] Tyson, Invitation to Christian Spirituality, p. 87.

was prepared by Antony's reflections on scripture and considering God's will for his life.

Antony developed a following and some members helped to support him as he battled demons and engaged in deep prayer in a cave high above a spring in the desert. He lived to age 105. When he was called upon he sometimes descended to the communities below to offer spiritual guidance.

How He Changed

Antony's life changed from that of a young, wealthy man to a life of poverty and simplicity. He adopted a life of constant prayer and seeking God with minimal worldly distractions.

Antony's conversion was dramatic. He suddenly felt called to a change of life when he heard the Gospel read in church, and he immediately took steps to bring about the change. He was not irresponsible in his planning – he took some time to arrange his affairs with his material goods and his family – but he left as soon as he could to find God in a solitary lifestyle.

How It Felt

This dramatic shift in his circumstances must have felt both freeing and frightening to Antony. Leaving everything he knew, and being alone without his parents, he launched into a new direction without much preparation. There is something thrilling about embarking on an adventure, but it could have been scary, too. Antony was resolute in his determination to stick it out as a solitary contemplative, or his wrestling with demons might have deterred him from his course.

Antony continued to love his sister because he provided for her, and he had compassion for people as evidenced by his willingness to engage the complex theological questions of his day. The bishop of Alexandria, Athanasius, had great respect for Antony's wisdom and called upon him when needed, and Antony responded to the call of his fellow men. He stayed compassionate and interested in the people around him while not allowing the affairs of the world to distract him from his solitary, contemplative call from God.

What You and I Can Do

From the life of Antony we can be inspired to be bold in our direction when we hear from God. Interior resonance with a scripture passage may be a word from Jesus to leave all and follow him. We see this in how Jesus called the apostles to follow him; they left their nets immediately, not looking back. Antony experienced something similar.

Another thing we can take away from Antony's conversion is that we do not need to be abrupt. The call of God will direct us. Antony moved in the direction God was leading him but he took the time to prepare his belongings and provide for the care of his sister. Even as a solitary monk Antony was available to respond to the needs of his community both as a spiritual guide and as a theological consultant to Church leaders such as St. Athanasius.

We should be alert to those who may want to learn from us. God has called us, and we have learned something about him and his ways, and in friendship with him, that could inspire and support others in their spiritual growth. Be free to share your experience and the word of your testimony with others.

Conclusion

By entering into the lives of the saints and the writings of the spiritual masters, we have seen how many different ways there are to change and grow closer to God. People grow spiritually through sudden insights from God, or step by step as God leads them toward himself by a gradual path that only he can see. We may make decisions to change our own lives or God may arrange the circumstances to show us his will. Some changes we might like, whereas others are distasteful or cause us to suffer due to giving up something we have loved.

Looking at the lives of the saints through their own writings, with a perspective on the changes they went through, has provided a sense of the various roads we may travel in our journeys toward God. We may hear God calling us gradually, suddenly or through circumstances, as we grow ever closer to him. May we continue our journey in light of the Truth, who is Jesus Christ. Amen.

Bibliography

Augustine. *Confessions.* Translated by R. S. Pine-Coffin. London: Penguin Books, 1961.

The Practice of the Presence of God. Edited by Conrad De Meester, O.C.D. Translated by Salvatore Sciurba, O.C.D. Washington DC: ICS Publications, 1994.

Chesterton, G. K. *Saint Francis of Assisi.* New York: Doubleday, 2001.

"Discerning the Voice of the Lord: Insights form Padre Pio's Testimony." September 11, 2023. https://capuchinswest.org/post-news/discerning-the-voice-of-the-lord-insights-form-padre-pios-testimony/.

Huntington, Anna. "The Holy Family Resting." https://osjusa.org/st-joseph/art/the-holy-family-resting/

Ignatius of Loyola, *Spiritual Exercises and Selected Works,* ed. George E. Ganss, S. J. (New York: Paulist Press, 1991), p. 70.

John Paul II. *Redemptoris Custos.* https://www.vatican.va/content/john-paul-ii/en/apost_exhortations/documents/hf_jp-ii_exh_15081989_redemptoris-custos.html.

Kavanaugh, Kieran, O.C.D. "The Book of Her Life – Introduction. *The Collected Works of St. Teresa of Avila,* Vol. 1. Washington DC: ICS Publications, 1987.

Le Tourneau, Dominique. *To Know St. Joseph: What Catholic Tradition Teaches about the Man Who Raised God.* El Cajon CA: Catholic Answers, 2021.

Mother Teresa. *Come Be My Light – The Private Writings of the Saint of Calcutta.* Edited by Brian Kolodiejchuk, M.C. New York: Doubleday, 2007.

Ruffin, C. Bernard. *Padre Pio: The True Story.* Huntington, IN: Our Sunday Visitor, 2018.

Spink, Kathryn. *Mother Teresa: An Authorized Biography.* New York: HarperCollins, 2011.

Teresa of Avila, *The Book of Her Life,* in *The Collected Works of St. Teresa of Avila,* Vol. 1. Tr. by Kieran Kavanaugh, O.C.D., and Otilio Rodriguez, O.C.D. Washington DC: ICS Publications, 1987. Ch. 32, 1-5.

Tyson, John R. "Introduction," in *Invitation to Christian Spirituality: An Ecumenical Anthology,* ed.

John R. Tyson. New York: Oxford University Press, 1999.

www.ingramcontent.com/pod-product-compliance
Lightning Source LLC
Chambersburg PA
CBHW060358050426
42449CB00009B/1789